I0409984

Iranian Regime Regional Threats

and

Strategic Responses

Walid Phares
July 2014

Copyright © 2012 Walid Phares

All rights reserved.

ISBN-10: 1500557307
ISBN-13: 937-1500557300

CONTENTS

PREFACE

Iraq Crisis
&
Iran Surfing on ISIS and Manipulating Washington

By Walid Phares

The ongoing crises in the Middle East, from Iraq to Gaza, and the destabilization of the Levant, the Arabian Peninsula and parts of North Africa are in large part created by the Islamic Republic of Iran. Tehran has meddled in its neighbor's affairs through the backing of terror networks. It has also seized a number of significant opportunities over the past five years to expand its military influence in the region, destabilize moderate Arab states, intervene in Syria, arm and train Hezbollah in Lebanon, threaten Bahrain, and back the Hawthi insurgents in northern Yemen. In 2009, the regime showed its true colors at home, too, cracking down on millions of citizens who were demonstrating peacefully against its policies. Tehran's most destructive role, however, can be most clearly distinguished in Iraq.

An analysis of the recent developments in Iraq would require a deeper exploration of the following questions:

- What are the causes of the recent crisis in Iraq?
- What is the solution to the crisis (and how can the ISIS threat be dealt with)?
- Can Iran be part of a potential solution to the Iraqi crisis?

The roots of the crisis in Iraq

The current situation in Iraq has been largely viewed by Iraq observers and international political figures as a by-product of the current Government of Nouri al-Maliki's sectarian and exclusionary policies. Maliki has enjoyed the backing of Tehran, which has also armed and trained sectarian paramilitary groups to advance its interests in Baghdad.

Embraced and supported by Tehran, Maliki's Government deprived nearly 10 million Sunnis of their most fundamental rights, purged them from many governmental agencies and the Army, arrested many of them under the pretext of fighting "terrorism", and as reported by watch groups, executed and killed thousands more. During Maliki's pro-Iranian tenure, Sunnis as well as have been completely marginalized and along with the Kurds excluded from the political process. Buoyed by promises of support from Tehran, Maliki's elite essentially monopolized power. The Baghdad Government also ignored a US-brokered agreement on power sharing that was reached in the city of Erbil in 2010. At the same time, Washington's position continued to be favorable to Maliki's Government as he gradually drifted towards Tehran.

In 2011, when Washington moved to withdraw its forces from Iraqi territory, it had a historic opportunity to leave the country in the hands of a coalition of moderates. For almost a decade, U.S. and Coalition Forces had largely succeeded in defeating the al-Qaeda threat, while pushing back against extremist groups in the south. Meanwhile the Kurds achieved local autonomy in the north. Moderate Shias, Sunnis and minorities were on the rise, and civil society NGOs were flourishing despite the sporadic episodes of terror and violence.

However, international lobbying by the Iranian regime—including, significantly, in the U.S.—coupled with significant pressures inside Iraq by pro-Iranian politicians convinced Washington to end its military presence while leaving central political institutions—including defense, security, and economic ministries—in the hands of a political party with deep ties to Tehran. From 2003 to 2009, Washington committed a fundamental mistake by failing to empower moderates and Iraqi civil society activists. As a result, instead of moderates forming an inclusive government capable of ending Iraq's misery and reintroducing it into the international fold, sectarian forces loyal to Tehran rose to power and steered the country toward even more violence. During 2009 to 2011, the single-most damaging strategic mistake committed by the U.S. administration was to partner with a pro-Iranian political elite in Iraq at the expense of all moderates.

By the time the unilaterally declared withdrawal from Iraq occurred at the end of 2011, Iraq had fallen into the hands of a government that was moving towards Tehran's sphere of influence. After the withdrawal, moderates were largely marginalized: Shia liberals, seculars and non-extremist religious factions were sidelined by the Maliki government. In a clear sign of Tehran's growing influence, Iraqi authorities carried out a violent attack against the main base of Iranian political exiles in Camp Ashraf, and forced its refugee population to evacuate it. Since then, Iraqi politics has been characterized by sectarianism and authoritarianism. When the early waves of the Arab Spring swept through Tunisia, Libya, Egypt and Syria, large segments of Iraq's civil society rose peacefully to protest against the authoritarian practices of the Maliki government, particularly against the Sunni community, only to face suppression. The parliamentary elections of 2010 gave the more moderate Shia coalition led by Iyad Allawi the largest number of seats in the Iraqi parliament. But after extensive Iranian pressure and Washington's acquiescence, Maliki's group was empowered and he was enabled to successfully secure a second term. The violent crackdown of Sunni tribes and politicians resumed, peaking in 2013. The Iraqi government's deliberate and systematic policy of excluding a large portion of the Iraqi population has forced many to rise up in protest.

Therefore, while a terrorist and extremist group, ISIS, has exploited the situation to expand its formal presence, it would certainly be a strategic mistake to downgrade a massive popular protest against a pro-Iranian Government in Baghdad to the escapades of a small terror group. The roots of the crisis point to a frankly legitimate and widespread grievance against the Maliki government. The solution to the crisis, then, lies in addressing those grievances.

Who is responsible for this development? In short, it is again the aggressive behavior of the Iranian regime and the influence it has acquired in Iraq, particularly since the U.S. withdrawal at the end of 2011, that is responsible for the failure of a pluralist and peaceful Iraq. In other word, the rise of Jihadi ISIS is the by-product of Iraqi government sectarian policies, Iran's meddling in Iraq and failure of U.S. policy on Iraq.

The political marginalization and physical annihilation of moderate Sunnis by pro-Iranian elements has enabled an extremely radicalized version of al Qaeda to take advantage of the broad resentment among the Sunni population. Iran was also instrumental in empowering ISIS across the border in Syria. By supporting the Assad regime, Iran and Hezbollah radicalized the peaceful uprising, and in fact enabled Jihadi militias. ISIS seized the momentum in Syria, fought moderate forces, thereby effectively aligning its short-term interests with Damascus and Tehran. Both Damascus and Tehran tolerated the limited presence of extremist groups in order to undermine the more moderate and determined Free Syrian Army. They gradually occupied large swathes of territory and finally stepped over the border into Iraq where they saw fertile ground for expansion.

Had the Iraqi government not been a surrogate to Iran's regime and a suppressor of Sunni moderates, it would have been the Sunni tribes of Iraq who would have blocked ISIS from penetrating into their country. Had Baghdad been governed by a coalition of the nationalist moderates with a mandate to create an inclusive government, the trajectory of events would perhaps have been radically different. Iran would not have enjoyed the extent of influence it now enjoys and ISIS could not find a fertile environment to expand.

Fighting ISIS

The real issue now is how to confront ISIS. Some argue that the U.S. must use its superior air power and bomb the group's positions. But as General David Petraeus has said the U.S. cannot be "the Air Force for Iraqi militia or a Shia on Sunni Arab fight." According to military experts, it is almost impossible to target ISIS without causing serious collateral damage. This has been made more difficult by the presence of local tribes and moderate Sunni forces who are also fighting the Iraqi government's forces.

Iran is in fact nudging the Administration towards military action because Washington's involvement in favor of the current government is in its long-term interest. First, the bombings will not only eradicate the security threat from ISIS, they will also strategically damage anti-government local tribes. Second, collateral damage as a result of American air strikes would incite anti-American sentiment. In the end, Tehran's position would be significantly strengthened in Baghdad to the detriment of U.S. national security interests in the region.

The most effective way to confront ISIS is to engage with tribes and the moderate Sunnis. In 2007, the United States successfully countered a similar al-Qaeda threat by working with moderate Sunni tribes and political figures. The backing of Sunni tribes was instrumental in the surge's success. Opening direct dialogue with the tribes recognizing their grievances, and inviting them back into the political process would encourage and enable them to defeat a much smaller ISIS. That would require the formation of a new Iraqi Government free from sectarian influences. The United States can help form a national unity government with representation from all sectors of the Iraqi population, including tribes and moderates. That approach would deny ISIS the fertile ground that it has thus far exploited.

The role of Iran

In view of what has been said above, Iranian influence in Iraq is clearly not constructive; it is destructive. Consequences would be catastrophic if Tehran succeeds in seducing Washington into cooperation or even silence. The active participation of the Iranian regime's Quds Force in the conflict in Iraq and its unhelpful interference in Iraq will further fan the flames of sectarianism.

The U.S. Government's de facto acceptance of Quds Force intervention in Iraq is fundamentally dangerous and an undoubted strategic mistake. Government and military officials have on numerous occasions stated that a large number of American soldiers in Iraq have been killed by Iranian trained and armed terrorist groups. So, it would be ironic, to say the least, for Washington to recognize, let alone coordinate and cooperate, with the Iranian regime or its Quds Force, which is incidentally designated as a foreign terrorist organization by the United States.

Tehran is in fact in breach of UN Security Council resolutions by sending arm shipments to the Iraqi government and its militias. Washington's position that "Iraq has the right to reach out to its neighbors for support" will prove to be a devastating lapse in judgment.

In conjunction with its attempts to increase its influence over Baghdad, Tehran is simultaneously trying to eliminate its main political opposition the Mujahedin-e Khalq, whose members now reside in Camp Liberty near Baghdad's international airport. By alleging that MEK has endorsed ISIS, it is feared that Tehran is setting the stage for another attack on Camp Liberty. The MEK has rejected the allegation. The mullahs' should know that these allegations would hardly be considered serious let alone believed, but they are hoping that by the way of propaganda, they can create a situation that there will be less attention on the plight of the people in Camp Liberty which the U.S. Government had pledged to protect.

It is indeed ironic that Tehran, long described by Washington as the foremost state sponsor of terrorism, is now claiming that it is at the forefront of the "war on terrorism" by assisting the Iraqi government in its fight against ISIS. Tehran is perhaps maneuvering to position itself as a legitimate player and a partner with the U.S. and the international community in the fight against al Qaeda and, now, ISIS. Some in Washington seem to be buying into this claim. In addition to several lobbying groups backing the Iranian regime, spokespersons for the Pentagon recently welcomed the idea that "Iraq's neighbors would be helping against ISIS."

Iran's strategic goal is to manipulate the United States administration so that the latter will bless Iranian intervention in Iraq on military and more subtle grounds. This would be catastrophic as it would grant Tehran right of passage to Iraq and, from Iraq, to the entire region If Iran is enabled in Iraq under the aegis of fighting ISIS, the regime will take advantage to support its own allies in Iraq empower at the expense of Shia moderates, whose presence is crucial for a new balanced government in Iraq, and will further alienate the Sunnis. Moreover, recognition of the Iranian regime's role inside Iraq will enable Tehran to move against the main opposition, thereby securing a strategic lifeline inside the country. At the same time, such a policy will endanger moderate U.S. allies in the Gulf, as Iran would be able to intimidate or target them for their alleged support of the Sunni insurgency in Iraq.

But perhaps the most dangerous impact of the U.S. recognition of Iran's influence in Iraq and of increased and exclusive support to the Maliki government would be seen on the ongoing nuclear negotiations. Six months after the November 2013 agreement, there seem to be little tangible outcomes in allaying western fears about the regime's pursuit of a nuclear weapon. Iran's Supreme Leader has given no indication that his regime will abandon that pursuit indefinitely. If the regime is granted a permanent and strategic foothold in Iraq on the grounds of fighting ISIS, it will certainly harden its position during nuclear negotiations and find itself in a more comfortable position to resume its pursuit of the bomb.

INTRODUCTION

The Iranian "nuclear deal" is on one hand the result of month—if not years—of under the table lobbying efforts to convince Washington that the Ayatollahs' regime is ready to do business with the United States and with the international community, particularly with regards to curbing its nuclear material production and its support to terror organizations in the region. On the other hand it is the result of the Iranian regime being engulfed in deep crisis which has made it desperate to reach a deal, hoping to buy some time and getting some concession from the West to overcome the crisis.[i]

Despite mounting evidence over the past few years that Tehran has been and continues to develop strategic weaponry systems and provides assistance and guidance to extremist groups in the Middle East and beyond, and in spite of the Islamic Republic's heavy involvement in Syria's bloody civil war, the U.S. administration decided to cut a deal with the Iranian regime, providing international support for the so-called agreement, and quickly engaged in transferring unfrozen Iranian funds to the government in Iran. Entrusting an Iranian regime controlled by the Supreme Leader and a powerful military and intelligence organization known as the "Islamic Revolutionary Guard of Iran" (IRGC) or "Pasdaran," itself on the U.S. terror list, with billions of dollars—and lifting economic sanctions and bestowing political recognition—may be the single most erroneous strategy decision made in Washington since 1979's crisis. [ii]

The "interim nuclear deal," which provides Tehran with a space for a global comeback in the international community, will backfire against regional and international security and eventually against U.S. national security and national interests. This assessment is shared by a wide scope of experts worldwide as well as governments and politicians in the Arab world. The focus should not be on attempts to affect the decision-making process of a rogue regime—as the declared goal of engaging the regime assumes. Had the engagement process been different, had it taken into consideration the ideology of the Ayatollahs' regime, its nerve center interests, the mechanics of its security and intelligence apparatus and also its international alliances—had the U.S. administration's attempt to impact the behavior of Iran's government been based on a partnership with an internal pressure by Iranian civil society and on a vigorous exiled opposition, principally the Mujahedin-e Khalq (MEK) which has shown to have roots and network in Iran and the broader coalition of National Council of Resistance of Iran (NCRI), then the process would have been positive, predictable and productive. The Iranian opposition was the source of revelation of the Iranian regime secret nuclear sites back in 2002. They could play a major role to make sure that if Iran attempt to dupe the West again, it revealed before it is too late.[iii]

Unfortunately, the so-called "nuclear deal," while it provides a narrative of relaxed tensions and of time-linked promises, the most basic of its components tells us that the regime will use the timeframe allowed by the "agreement" and the material gratifications offered as implementation of the "deal" to position the regime in a context much more dangerous than the one that preceded the conclusion of the interim settlement.[iv]

These serious developments, which will provide opportunity for the regime to get out of the current crisis, increasing abilities to the Khomeinist regime to further develop its strategic capacities, a deeper suppression of its own population and push the region to the brink of more dramatic disasters, must be addressed by the public in the United States, across the free world, and primarily by members of the U.S. Congress and the European Parliament. The pressing nature of the current developments deserves a comprehensive assessment of the "deal" in light of several decades of Iranian regime behavior, of the post 9/11 U.S. strategies regarding this regime—particularly the five past years of handling the Iranian threat. In fact, the rapid regaining of strength by the ruling elite in Tehran due to the ongoing influx of cash from the U.S. and the West and the gradual collapse of the sanctions requires immediate measures to stop the current erroneous process. These efforts should be redirected toward obtaining guaranteed strategic results—starting with the elimination of the nuclear armed threat emanating from the Islamic Republic and ending with an empowerment of the Iranian people. The outcome must be the replacement of this repressive regime with a representative democracy which would not constitute a threat to its neighbors and the region and would cease the brutalization of its own population.[v]

This paper is a contribution to the strategic analysis of Iran's global threats, the regime's increasing role in destabilization in the Greater Middle East and adjacent regions, and the consequences of an engagement process which will fortify the regime and trigger much greater dangers in the region. The paper will also briefly analyze the regimes weaknesses and how best that could be utilized for a fundamental change in Iran. Accordingly, the paper will suggest appropriate alternative policies to the current "deal," namely a road map to regime change in Tehran.

1. The first section will remind the reader of the historic ideological and political roots of the present Iranian regime and underline that its original goals and its final objectives have not changed—and that the regime's central nerve power has kept up a relentless march towards these goals.

2. The paper will then examine the Iranian involvement in Syria's civil war and the destructive role it has been playing since 2011. This will be followed by the Iranian meddling in Iraq and the suppressive campaign against Iran's exiled opposition in that country.

3. The paper will analyze the Iranian obstruction of solutions in Syria and Iraq along with the support Tehran is providing to terror forces in both countries before discussing the role of Iranian-backed Hezbollah in Lebanon.

4. Discussing the Iranian opposition as the strategic Achilles' heel of the Iranian regime

5. Last will come a discussion of the misguided U.S. policy on Syria and Iraq, particularly that, under the pretext the government will confront al Qaeda, Assad is allowed to continue with his genocide and Maliki is allowed to perform the bidding of Iran.

The conclusion will offer policy suggestions regarding the containment of Iran's regime and alternative strategies for Iraq and Syria. Most of these themes have been repeated time and again by many other experts or journalists, but what has been lacking is a vision for solutions. This paper will offer guidelines for a comprehensive strategy to achieve a resolution to this regional and international quagmire. Solutions will be based on a better understanding of the threat posed by Tehran's regime, incorporate the flexibility to endure and grow, and address the flaws in the strategies in play since the "Iran nuclear deal" was enacted. However, the heart of this solution is to rely on the Iranian people and opposition for change, a factor that has been absolutely absent in the US and Western policy on Iran over the past 35 years. The alternative road map has not yet been tested, and this paper is an attempt to provide convincing arguments for the public, lawmakers and researchers to consider and adopt. [vi]

Iran's regime history: A reminder

When decision makers and strategists design their policies regarding regimes such as Iran, in addition to geopolitical considerations, economic and security interests, they must factor in the historical roots and evolution of the regime since its inception (in Iran's case, that is 1979). From Beirut and as a contemporary observer of the Islamic revolution—witnessing its evolution since its first days and monitoring its impact on the region, including its effect on Syria, Lebanon, Iraq and many other countries—I have established in my three-decades-long research that the Khomeini's regime has been systematic and relentless in its search for power and expansion in the Middle East. Having had many articles and analyses published in Beirut, Europe and, for more than 24 years, in the United States, I have closely followed the long term strategic agenda of the regime under Ayatollah Khomeini and his successor Ayatollah Khamenei regarding the Islamic Republic's strategic weapons, geopolitical designs and ideological objectives. The depth and breadth of my work and the observations that have led to it are enough to establish the behavior, narrative and actions of this regime, the fundamental principles driving its leading elites, have not changed. Rather, they have solidified and in their own perception have become closer than ever to realization. In 1987, I published a book in Arabic titled *Qira'atfi al Thawra al Khumeiniya: al Jumhuriya al Islamiya, Khalfiyat wa abaad.* (Readings in the Khomeinist Revolution: The Islamic Republic, Backgrounds and Projections). [vii] In it, I argued that the eight year-old revolution was not a nationalist, patriotic and social revolt, but was at some point seized by a highly ideological fundamentalist faction, which developed a long term strategic agenda, one that would take decades to implement. The book projected the Tehran regime's aim to expand outside its borders into Iraq, Syria, Lebanon, and the Arabian Peninsula and to shield these ambitions through establishing a mass destruction weapons system aimed at deterring outside forces from challenging this regime. In 1991, I warned in an article published in *Global Affairs* in Washington, D.C., of a long term alliance between Tehran and Damascus in what I titled "The Syrian-Iranian

Axis." The regional axis included the two regimes in control of Iran and Syria, Hezbollah in Lebanon, and Iraq's pro-Iranian opposition. [viii]

In the 1980s, in addition to projecting Tehran's long term strategy, my work specified that strategy which would aim to equip the regime with strategic weapons—nuclear and other mass casualty arms—as well as their means of delivery, such as long range missiles. Under the bipolar world with two superpowers dividing the Middle East in zones of influence, Khomeini's elite sought to survive the clash between the East and the West as it promoted itself as a third force in the region. "No East, no West, one Islamic Umma," chanted his supporters in the 1980s. The Islamic Republic, even though isolated geopolitically during that decade, thought of itself as a legitimate representative of the entire "Islamic Umma" against both evils—the American Satan and the Soviet Satan—while considering Israel as the small Satan in the region. The doctrinal political philosophy of the Iranian Islamist regime, which produced the commitment to the military nuclear choice, was also reinforced by the destructive war with Saddam Hussein (1980-1987). Tehran's elite believed regional wars on its borders might jeopardize its interests—if not its survival—and that the weapon that would most decisively protect those interests would be of a nuclear nature. Hence, since its inception, the regime has pursued weapons of mass destruction—including nuclear weapons—as part of its strategic goals. Current discussion in Geneva and the surrounding assessments in Western capitals about the possible Iranian abandonment of the military nuclear choice are simply ignorant of the historical root of the Islamic Republic. The bomb and its delivery system have been goals of the Khomeinists since the earliest years of the Islamist theocracy. They became part of their ideological and geopolitical raison d'etre in the same manner the technological military advancements of the Soviet Union or the Third Reich were part of their political philosophies leading to destructive wars and inhuman suppression of populations.

The 1980s also signaled an historic alliance between Tehran and Damascus as they signed agreements binding them together militarily, politically, economically and on the level of intelligence sharing and cooperation. And under this axis, Iran's Revolutionary Guard, the Pasdaran, penetrated Lebanon via Syria and connected with militant Shia militias, coaching them to form what later became Hezbollah. Initially formed in the northern Bekaa, Hezbollah was backed financially and militarily by Iran as it pushed into the country until it controlled most of the south, the Bekaa, and Beirut's southern suburbs. Hezbollah waged a terror war against American and French peacekeeping units in Lebanon and launched suicide attacks and car bombings on Western interests until the multinational forces evacuated the country, leaving Lebanon for Assad-Hezbollah forces to obliterate. That opportunity came in 1990 when—in a strategic mistake—the United States and its allies, outmaneuvered by the Iranians and the Syrians, gave permission to Assad and *his* allies to invade the last free enclave of the country still defended by the Lebanese Army. Iran and Syria's regime then established joint control or a "condominium" over Lebanon. Tehran's span of control, just ten years after its Islamic revolution, covered three countries: Iran, Syria and Lebanon. [ix]

In the 1990s, with the collapse of the Soviet Union, the Islamic Republic saw an historic opportunity to advance its strategic goals on two fronts. As the USSR vanished, a greater space of influence opened for Tehran in the region. Iraq was no longer backed by Moscow, particularly after the debacle of Kuwait in 1991. The Soviet Empire dismantled, and the Russian Federation practically abandoned Saddam, leaving the Khomeinists to absorb parts of his Shia opposition and prepare for the next opportunity to remove the Iraqi regime. That decade, Tehran's momentum in pursuit of its regional and international agenda increased sharply.[x]

Inside Iran, the regime maintained its severe repression for a second decade against its opposition, including students, ethnic minorities, liberal figures and particularly the components of the national armed resistance known as Mujahidin Khalq, many of whom have taken exile in neighboring Iraq. After his defeat in Kuwait, Saddam Hussein's ability to confront Iran had all but vanished, opening the door for Tehran to organize anti-Saddam refugees inside Iran. These elements would become the core of the groups who would return to Iraq and serve as a beachhead for Iran's penetration that began in 2003.

With the collapse of the Soviet Union, the Islamic Republic stepped in to replace the great power as a regional ally and financial and military backer of the Assad regime. The early cooperation of the 1980s expanded into full strategic control of Lebanon, and with Hezbollah, Syria and Iran engaged in international operations of penetration, from the Arab world to parts of Africa—to Latin America. In the early 1990s, Iran and Hezbollah perpetrated terror attacks in Argentina to send a strong message to the U.S. in its own hemisphere after the bombings of the Marine Barracks in Beirut in 1983. And with the Khobar towers in Saudi Arabia, Iran entered the fray of entanglements in the Arabian Peninsula. Back in Lebanon, Hezbollah waged relentless operations from south Lebanon against Israel and its local Lebanese allies to affirm its control of the East Mediterranean nation. By 2000, Israel withdrew and Hezbollah, read Iran, reached the northern international borders with Israel. During that same decade, Iran's intelligence and Hezbollah recruited terror group Hamas to become an extension of Khomeinist power in Gaza, reaching not only Israel's southern border, but also technically Egypt's eastern border. The 1990s was the decade where Iran's regime maximized its geopolitical reach in the region—reaching the Mediterranean and deploying terror organizations in Lebanon and Gaza. [xi]

As the third decade of the Islamist regime ended, the country was forced to address a challenging development generated by the 9/11 attacks by al Qaeda against the U.S. homeland. America, and with it the West, was awakening to the threat of terrorism. The mass casualties inflicted on U.S. soil in 2001 mobilized the American public like never before. The Iranian-sponsored attacks against the Marines barracks and the U.S. embassy in the early 1980s did not enflame average citizens as al Qaeda's carnage in New York and in Washington did. Americans were ready to wage war on terrorists, and Iran's regime felt it may be on the U.S. target list as of that year. American forces crumbled the Taliban regime in neighboring Afghanistan shortly after. While the Sunni extremist regime was a competitor to the Mullahs, its fall was a signal that times might be very dangerous for the Islamic Republic. A Western force thrust to central Asia, east of Iran, and took out an Islamist regime. The State of the Union Address by President Bush in January 2002 named Iran as one of the Axis of Evil members, prompting more concerns about possible action against Tehran's power or one of its allies in the region—the Syrian regime or Hezbollah. In March 2003, the U.S. invaded Iraq, toppled Saddam Hussein and set up the foundations for a new government. Iran's elite was not mourning Saddam, but it was watching its neighborhood transform while NATO forces surrounded the regime from the East and the West. It is not a coincidence that Iran's regime declared stopping its nuclear program that same year.

That move was not generated by an internal reform within the regime, but inspired by the repetitive U.S. offensives in the region. Tehran's strategists read the geopolitical changes accurately. The U.S. and its allies had taken down two dictatorships, encircled the country, and Washington had labeled the Iran as evil. More perturbing for Tehran was a Franco-American move the following year which obtained a UN Security Council Resolution calling on Syria to withdraw from Lebanon and Hezbollah to disarm. Khamenei's elite read this move on its allies in the region as the last step before a possible action against the Islamic Republic. In March 2005, a popular revolt known as the "Cedars Revolution" exploded in Beirut. It was immediately backed by Washington and Paris and was followed by a pullout of Syrian forces from the country. This last pro-Western offensive against Iran's allies occurred just months before Ahmadinejad came to power in June. From there on, a counteroffensive began in the region. In Lebanon, Hezbollah waged an assassination campaign against the Cedars Revolution politicians. In Iraq, the pro-Iranian militias put pressure on the U.S. led bureaucracy to accept a greater role for politicians with closer ties to Tehran. And in the Gulf, Iran's intelligence manipulated Shia militants to destabilize the Arab allies of the United States.

By 2006 Iran's nuclear program was back on the table. Khamenei and his assistants—as as well as Ahmadinejad—reaffirmed their right to nuclear energy while at the same time claiming their right to strategic arms to defend themselves against perceived enemies. Between 2006 and 2013, the Iranian regime moved forward on all fronts to reassert its initial strategy of nuclear weapons and regional expansions. In Lebanon in 2006, Hezbollah ignites a war with Israel at the end of which the terror organization gained momentum and strength, prompting it to wage an urban war against its Lebanese opposition in May 2008, allowing them to since seize Lebanon's national security apparatus. In Gaza, Hamas booted Fatah out of the enclave in 2007 and asserted its exclusive authority, projecting Iranian power south of Israel. By 2009, Iran's allies in Northern Yemen the Hawthis were waging guerilla warfare against both Sanaa's government and the Saudis. Despite sanctions expanded by the Bush administration throughout the first decade of the new millennium, Iran continued to work on its military nuclear program and its missiles systems. The aggressive attitude of the Iranian regime deepened even further after President Barack Obama sent its letter regarding "open dialogue" with the Islamic republic in June 2009.

The Obama's Administration new policy towards Iran

When President Obama sent his open letter to the Islamic Republic Guide Ayatollah Khamenei in 2009 seeking "dialogue" and "engagement," the regime in Tehran understood it as abandonment by the new administration of policies always upheld by its predecessors, particularly with regard to isolating Tehran internationally. The June letter was the first element in a U.S. diplomatic change towards the Ayatollahs and the latter's motivation to push deeper towards strategic arming and regional expansion. As Washington engaged the regime before a meaningful change or reform could take place in Tehran, it provided the Islamic Republic with an incentive to solidify its position—not to moderate it. A regime that has maintained ideological consistency over several decades is more definitive in its pursuit to accomplish its ultimate goals than to address what the Obama administration was seeking to accomplish. The change of policy toward the Islamic Republic was seen by Iran Washington "blinking" in the long face to face stare down between the two sides that has been taking place since the Cold War. The letter from Obama encouraged the Ayatollahs to move forward toward their ultimate agenda, not to walk back their intentions. It was a strategic mistake on behalf of the United States to signal to the Islamic Republic that they had hope for a massive change of policy in Iran while in reality the only change that was to happen was a change toward more assertiveness and aggressiveness on behalf of the regime.[xii]

The second immediate political stance by Washington during that same month was to ignore the mass uprising that took place in Tehran and other cities as a result of the manipulated election results renewing the presidency to Mahmoud Ahmadinejad. The statement by President Obama, refusing to officially support the demonstrators so that the United States "are not seen as meddling in Iran's affairs," was the declaration that convinced the Iranian decision makers that the United States would no longer intervene to back revolts against the ruling order. The new revelation was immense in its political value as it proved to the Ayatollahs and their Pasdaran force that future revolts would not find American—

and therefore Western—backing and thus the Iranian opposition, including the organized opposition of the MEK and its allies in the NCRI, have been abandoned (more will be said on the opposition in the next section). The reaction by the regime forces on the ground and the brutal repression of youth, among them the young girl Nada killed by Bassij snipers, signaled a decision by the regime to crush the revolt, known in the media as "Green Revolution," and suppress future uprisings. The internal movement aimed at reforming or, at best, changing the regime, found itself abandoned by the outside world and left to struggle for its own survival.[xiii]

The two U.S. attitudes, engaging the regime and abandoning civil society, gave an impetus to the regime to go after the most organized corps of the opposition: the national resistance movement headquartered in Paris—with a significant presence in Iraq. The National Council of the Iranian Resistance, known also as Mujahidin Khalq, is perceived by the regime as its fiercest and worse enemy. Centralized, well organized and knowledgeable about the power centers of the regime, the NCIR has a long history of opposing the Pasdaran. Profiting from an American lethargy towards Iran since 2009, Tehran mobilized its allies in Iraq to strike at Camp Ashraf, the largest gathering of Iranian refugees outside their country, organized by the NCIR. Iran's regime pressured the Baghdad Government of M. Nouri Maliki to encircle the camp and dismantle it. Thanks to international support, Ashraf resisted for two more years before it was eventually shut down and its residents removed to other locations in Iraq. In 2013 and 2014, a number of Iranian exiles in Iraq were killed, tortured and jailed. Tehran was eliminating its strongest opposition in the region, essentially eliminating potential future struggle for regime change.[xiv]

Iranian involvement in Syria's civil war

In 2011, when the Arab Spring exploded from Tunisia to Egypt, Arab youth were partially inspired by the young Iranians demonstrating against the regime in Tehran in 2009 and by the young Lebanese who demonstrated against the pro-Iranian Syrian occupation of Lebanon in 2005. The anti-Khomeinist resistance in the region, at least in the Levant, in fact revealed the path of revolution to the Arab world. The Arab Spring learned from the Iranian and the Lebanese peoples, not just in terms of revolutionary principles, but also in terms of urban demonstration tactics. The Iranian regime was right to fear its own opposition—and even more the Iranian resistance movement. The Mullahs knew that these democratic forces are the ones qualified and capable of performing regime change in Tehran. Thus they suppressed any such forces, both inside the country and across their borders. And the U.S. engagement policy, which started effectively in the Spring of 2009 and continued to progress until the "Iranian nuclear deal" of 2013, allowed the Iranian regime to survive its own democratic forces, as well as the winds of change released by the Arab Spring, and to eventually get involved in a series of wars waged by its allies in the region against their own peoples.

Indeed, in the Spring of 2011, Tehran sided with authoritarian forces in the Levant as civil societies in the Arab world emulated each other uprisings from Tunisia to Yemen, from Egypt to Syria. While North Africa appears to have been outside the direct reach of Iran (and has endured the control of the Islamist Sunni movements, at least in Tunisia, Libya and Egypt), the Near East collapsed in the hands of Iran's allies as uprisings escalated. Syria, the home of a popular revolt beginning in March 2011, was the target of significant Iranian intervention. As children and women triggered the first demonstrations in the southern city of Der'a in the early Spring, Assad security forces launched a violent repressive campaign against the protestors. In just few weeks, the Iranian intelligence and security apparatus were operating inside Syria to back the regime against the popular explosion. As in Iran, the U.S. administration missed an opportunity to side quickly and efficiently with civil society before the country fell into a ravaging and extremely bloody civil war.[xv]

The Iranian intervention in Syria was predictable at the onset of the conflict in early 2011. As I argued in my 1991 *Global Affairs* journal article, "The Syrian-Iranian Axis," the alliance between the two regimes of Ayatollah Khomeini and President Hafez Assad was grounded by two major roots. One, perceived as sectarian, brought together an Islamist Iranian regime claiming it defends the Shia community worldwide and a Syrian regime perceiving itself as a defender of the Alawi minority, an offshoot of Shi'ism. The other root, however, may have been the deeper reason for the historic alliance between the two regimes. The Khomeinists imposed themselves on their own people by way of violence and perpetuated their control by way of oppression. As with the fascist regimes of the 1930s in Europe, the Iranian regime's survival against an uprising hinges on finding constant outside enemies and attempting to expand in the region—thus creating an atmosphere of perpetual warfare with these perceived enemies. The Arab countries, Israel and the West, including mainly the United States, were relentlessly portrayed as the foes who wanted the destruction of Iran as a nation, allowing the Iranian government in the beginning of its inception to mobilize the public against a windmill of enemies and for many years now mobilizing and uniting its own suppressive forces, namely the IRGC and paramilitary elements such as the Basijis. The Assad regime built a similar vision of resisting aggressors against Syria and the Arabs. From the "Zionist enemy" to the "isolationists in Lebanon," to the U.S. and Arab Gulf states, Hafez, then Bashar Assad since 2000, tightened control over the Syrian people by claiming they were defending the country against an outside enemy. Hence, Tehran and Damascus found themselves as two regimes fighting almost the same enemies and defending their peoples and the "Umma" against aggression. Assad's Umma were the Arabs, and Khomeini's Umma were Muslims worldwide. Iran and Syria's ruling elites did not mention the Shia factor as an official reason for their alliance, rather they focused on the "enemy" to confront, mostly Israel and often the United States. [xvi]

In the 1980s, Hezbollah—backed by both Iran and Syria—waged a bloody campaign against a U.S. presence in Lebanon. Iranian revolutionary guards have been present on Lebanese soil since 1981, using Syria's ports and airports to enter Lebanon. The Iranian intelligence apparatus has been deployed in both countries for several decades. After the Cold War, the Iranian regime assets in Lebanon grew stronger and reinforced their presence in Syria.[xvii] In 2005, as the Syrian military withdrew from the country, the Iranian presence increased—the embassy stood as its headquarters, but there was a presence in several parts of Lebanon. During the 2006 war with Israel, the coordination between Hezbollah and Syria via the Iranian security apparatus demonstrated the efficiency of an integrated three way war room. Over recent years, if not decades previous, Iran, Syria and Hezbollah have established a regionally sized joint war room, which they have used to defend the three regimes against their enemies and to conduct terror operations in the Middle East and around the world. During the American led

Coalition presence in Iraq, the joint war room brought Hezbollah operatives to Iraq, and Syria intelligence facilitated the passage of Jihadists across its own borders with Iraq. When the revolt exploded in Syria in 2011, it should have been evident and predictable that the "joint war room" would mobilize its full capabilities to support the Assad regime. Iranian support to Syria can only be compared to Hitler's support of Mussolini during WWII.

In the early months of the Syrian unrest, the Assad regime used its security and intelligence services, Mukhabart, to suppress the demonstrations, particularly in the south, around Damascus and in some parts of the northwest. Soon thereafter, the regime deployed its own Baathist militia, known as the "Shabiha" or "thugs," to perform assassinations, tortures and mass arrests. Hezbollah and Iran's assets were available but not yet significantly utilized in battle. The year was critical, as U.S. forces were still operational in Iraq and along the borders. The war room assessment was to wait diligently for the full pullout of American personnel from Iraq so there would be no danger of U.S. military being used against the Syrian regime as President Obama's statement about the necessity for Assad to step down was read as a possible signal toward U.S. and Western intervention in Syria in the same manner NATO intervened in Libya. The Iranian and Syrian regimes were careful as to avoid any trigger for such use before the last day of December 2011. Massive assistance from Iran and Hezbollah was off the table, and the Syrian air force was not sent to the battle, with the exception of a limited use of helicopters. However, with the completion of a U.S. withdrawal from Iraq by early 2012, the "axis" gradually moved on the offensive.[xviii]

During 2012, the United States was engulfed with its presidential elections, a time where it is difficult to achieve domestic consensus regarding international massive interventions. The Syrian regime in coordination with Iran's Pasdaran invited Hezbollah to send its intelligence service as well as urban guerilla specialists to assist Syria's Special Forces as they sought to violently counter the opposition. The latter, having despaired of U.S. and Western interventions, militarized. The early stages of the armed resistance were organized by Syrian military dissidents, who that year formed the Free Syria Army (FSA). By midyear, Pasdaran elite units were transferred from Iran to Syria via Iraq territories or airspace. The Iranian Revolutionary Guards were deployed to protect defense and strategic centers, including missile sites and WMD systems. Observers dispatched from the U.S. spotted these Pasdaran sites in Eastern Syria and reported the military land bridge from Iran to Syria through the Shia majority areas of Iraq. The war room was careful not to deploy the Iranian reserve forces inside Sunni zones in Syria, for fear of being identified and caught, because of their Farsi language. But the war room deployed larger units of Lebanese Hezbollah and Iraqi militias operating under the Maliki government in areas controlled by the Syrian regime and used in attacks against Sunni rebels. The Iraqi-Lebanese Hezbollah expeditionary corps was Iran's advanced division inside Syria's civil war. At the end of 2012 and throughout 2013, the "Iranian army"—comprised of Hezbollah, Iraqi militias and Pasdaran—entered the fray of the Syrian war on several fronts and was given appropriate weapons, large-scale ammunition and, most importantly, access to heavier Syrian weapons, including armor, artillery and missiles. The "Iranian Army of Syria" became the equivalent of the Nazi SS Corps in occupied Europe and later in Italy in 1944. The power center of the "axis," Tehran in this sense, is not "intervening" in Syria; in fact, it is omnipresent to defend its suzerain regime, Assad's. [xix]

Operationally, by early 2013 the Iranian military and intelligence complex was taking command of the joint operations on Syrian soil. In other words, Tehran was commanding the battlefields across Syria against the FSA and other militias. The architect of Iraq's chaos, General Qassem Suleimani, who heads the infamous Quds force inside the Pasdaran, played an important role in implanting Iranian command centers inside Syria. After having lost many of his officers to the opposition, and having experienced assassination attempts against his own military general staff, Bashar Assad conceded most of the strategic command and control of major military operations in Syria to the Iranians who have a direct web of communications with the Alawi and pro-Assad sectors of the Syrian Army, Pasdaran units, Iraqi militias, Hezbollah and other Lebanese armed groups operating on Syrian soil. Technically, the war in Syria is fought from the war room of the Pasdaran/Quds force in Tehran. [xx]

Iranian intervention in Syria increased qualitatively and quantitatively during the summer of 2013 and into the fall of that year—before and after the battle of Qussair where Hezbollah led the counteroffensives and won the day. Syria's military opposition had seized the strategic city of Qussair in order to cut communications between Damascus and the Alawite enclave in the northwest. When the regular Syrian army appeared unable to take back the city, Iran's central command ordered Hezbollah into the battle. Despite significant losses, the "Party of Allah" took the location back using Syrian tanks and artillery. Throughout 2013, the Syrian regime was saved and consolidated with the help of Iran's "expeditionary force." [xxi]

The Iranian intervention in Syria, unlike how some describe it as a support to Assad in return for the alliance between the two regimes, is more of an Iranian strategic regional project. As we underlined earlier, the Khomeinist agenda has always been to expand the Islamic revolution in all directions possible to form a global Islamist power—to become an Imamate. The establishment of an Imamate would be a manifestation of a doctrinal vision established by the Velayat-e Faqih: seeking a world empire for the service of the divine. Both assertions— mutual alliance and spiritual service—serve only to legitimize more geopolitical interests. The rulers of Tehran desire to maintain a continuum of influence from Iran to the Eastern Mediterranean, encompassing Iraq, Syria and Lebanon, with an enclave in Gaza. Syria is the strategic passage from Iran to the Mediterranean via Iraq. If the Assad regime falls, the Khomeinist project in the region would lose a major component for further expansion. If Syria ceases to be an Iranian ally, Hezbollah will be isolated in Lebanon and eventually neutralized by Syrians and the Lebanese. Iran wo uld lose its principal international arm for terror tactics and propaganda. Furthermore, if Assad leaves Damascus, a mostly Sunni-based regime will seize power. This could lead to two damaging futures for the Iranians. First, a non-Alawi Syria would naturally sympathize with the Sunnis of Iraq and endanger Iran's Iraqi ally, Nour al Maliki or his successor. A weakening of the pro-Iranian Shia leadership in Baghdad would bring the pressure back to Iran's borders along with a high possibility that Iranian exiles would reorganize and again threaten the Ayatollahs. Another projection emanating from a defeat of Assad points toward a new Syria in alliance with Jordan, Saudi Arabia, and most of the Gulf striking back at the Islamic Republic. In short, an Iranian defeat in Syria would unleash a domino effect all the way into the heart of the regime in Tehran. The Iranian elite in power cannot afford to lose Syria. The matter is not about Iranian faithfulness to Assad but about maintaining Iranian control of Syria. Thus, Iran's regime will fight for the Assad regime and will not back off on Syria.[xxii]

Iran's Iraq onslaught

If Tehran considers Syria as a strategic regional project, it considers Iraq as a pillar of Iran's national and regional security. As I argued in many briefings to Congress and in articles and interviews, the Khomeinists gave priority in their regional push to the countries with a Shia majority. Claiming to be the world center of Shi'ism, the rulers of Tehran and Qum kept a close eye on Iraq and its large Shia community. After eliminating the democracy forces in the anti-Shah coalition, the first goal of the Islamist coup of 1979 was to control Iraq. Even though, chronologically, Iraq was the third country to fall to the Ayatollahs, after Lebanon and Syria, it nevertheless was always one of the highest priorities for the rulers of the Islamic Republic. Indeed, though it was Saddam Hussain who invaded Iran in September 1980, but a deep look into the events of the time show that it was Khomeini who laid the seeds for the start of the war with Iraq by publically calling on the Iraqi people to revolt against Saddam.

The Khomeinist institution of Velayat-e Faqih is based on the assumption that the Supreme Leader of the revolution is the top representative of the divine on Earth and that all political and constitutional institutions of Iran are under the guide's power and control. The very foundation of the Iranian regime rests on the assumption that the Shia world is ruled by the Faqih. His orders are not discussed by elected representatives, and his office is higher than that of the president, the cabinet and the parliament. Such an exclusive divine source of legitimacy provides unlimited power to the head of the regime and to his security agencies. But Iraq's Shia traditions are among the oldest, if not the first in the world. Karbala', Najaf and other *Maqamat* (religious sites) represent the birthplaces of Shi'ism. They are to Shia worldwide what Jerusalem, Nazareth and Bethlehem are to Christians. Thus, supreme spiritual leaders emerging from Iraq could compete with the Iranian scholars and religious leaders of Qum and Mashad in Iran. Ironically, as long as the Iraqi Shiites were under Saddam's domination, the Khomeinists announced themselves as the top spiritual leaders of the Shia worldwide and condemned the Baathist Sunni leader as a brutal dictator suppressing their brothers in religion. But when the U.S. Coalition invaded Iraq and toppled Saddam Hussein, the Shia community was freed from Pan Arab Sunni domination and entered a stage dangerous for the Khomeinists. Iraq's Shia, the largest group in the country, were rising and preparing to become major players in the future of Iraq. The risk of having Iraqi moderate spiritual leadership, like Grand Ayatollah Sistani, or even Shia moderate politicians, coming to government in Baghdad would have threatened Tehran's "Shia model." Thus Iran's regime introduced its own "Iraqi Shia politicians," a card it had prepared to play decades ago.[xxiii]

Indeed, since the inception of the Iranian Islamic revolution in 1979, one of the priorities of the Khomeinist regime immediately after the elimination of the moderate and secular elements of the revolution inside Iran and in exile was to penetrate the spiritual and later the political leadership of the Shia community of Iraq. The target of Tehran—after consolidating the new Islamist Republic—was to topple their neighbor's government and establish an Islamist regime in Iraq with the help of pro-Khomeinist allies inside Iraq's Shia community. Iran's intelligence was able to enlist several waves of Iraqi Shia exiles who took refuge inside Iranian territory when fleeing Saddam. The Iraqi opposition in exile in Iran was the prime ally of the regime whilst waiting for an historic opportunity to move to Baghdad. Another consideration that mobilized Tehran to seize influence and power in Iraq was the negative effects an Iranian opposition in exile across the borders could have inside the country.[xxiv]

The Iranian regime worked patiently during the Iran-Iran war of 1980-1988, and then again after the Iraq invasion of Kuwait and the subsequent Saddam defeat and retreat, to enlist Iraqi Shia cadres. In the wake of a massive repression of the Shia who rose against Saddam in 1991 as a result of President George H.W. Bush's call on "all Iraqis to rise," many Shia leaders and militants escaped to Iran where they were hosted, supported and aided in organizing militias and networks. Among the pro-Iranian opposition forces were the Badr Brigade, the Supreme Islamic Council and others. This "Iraqi pro-Iranian force" was among the first returnees to Iraq as a result of the U.S. invasion and toppling Saddam Hussein. In five years, even under Coalition administration, the pro-Iranian groups succeeded in establishing themselves as unavoidable forces in Iraqi politics. While alternative Shia political voices were trying to carve a space for themselves in Iraqi politics, the pro-Iranian groups and politicians had the upper hand. One major reason for the success of the pro-Iranian Iraqis over the moderate Iraqis came from the several serious mistakes made by the U.S. administrators of Iraq—first under the Bush administration and more so under the Obama administration. It would have been the equivalent of U.S. managers of West Germany favoring the Communists instead of the liberals during the Cold War as a way to accommodate the Soviet Union. In other words, the Iranian regime was able to position his political allies in Iraq, first within the U.S. occupation administration, and then through policymakers in Washington. With time, and as moderate Shiite politicians were sidelined in parliament and pushed back by the pro-Iranian hardliners, the web of Iranian intelligence, the pro-Iranian militias and politicians were able to secure control over the community and seize much of the Iraqi bureaucracy and government power. By 2008, Iran's networks were established deep within Iraq, controlling the community's major players, intimidating Sunni politicians, and keeping the Kurdish leaders at bay. One major concern the Iranian regime had in Iraq was the elimination of anti-Khomeinist bases of Iranian exiles inside the country under MEK's auspices, particularly Camp Ashraf. Attacks against the center took place even as U.S. forces were still in the country. [xxv]

In 2009, as U.S. policy changed towards the Middle East and Iran, after President Obama's letter was received by Ali Khamenei, and after the abandonment of Tehran's demonstrators in June, pro-Iranian activities surged in Iraq on all fronts: More influence in government, more contacts with the Iranian military and security leaders, and escalation against the anti-Iranian regime groups inside Iraq. The commitment made by the Obama administration to pull out of Iraq by the end of 2011 became a roadmap for the Iranian regime to strategically move into Iraq. Unfortunately, two U.S. administrations failed to transform Iraq's campaign into a strategic victory. The Bush administration was strong in its determination to fight al Qaeda and push back against the Iranian influence. What it failed to achieve was the construction of an appropriate anti-Khomeinist coalition in Iraq. Instead of isolating the pro-Iranian elements in the country and backing a multiethnic political coalition with liberal Shia, moderate Sunnis and Kurds, Christians and other minorities, it allowed the allies of Iran to manipulate Iraqi politics with the help of Iranian petrodollars and radical militias, like Sadr's Mahdi Army and other extremist militias. The second mistake of the Bush administration was its failure to build—inside Iraq and along the borders with Iran—a vast network of Iranian opposition groups, camps and broadcast media and support them in their interactions with the opposition inside Iran. Instead of one Camp Ashraf, there should have been many; and there should have been TV and radio stations supporting the cause. By the time an internal uprising was to happen in Iran, the Iranian community exiled in Iraq would have been to Iran what General De Gaulle was to France in 1944 while based in England. On the contrary the US called on the Iranian opposition to disarm which was certainly a gift to the Iranian regime.[xxvi]

From when the Obama administration took over in 2009 until the full pull out in 2011, the Iranian influence in Iraq grew deeper, and the Maliki government provided more opportunities to the pro-Iranian factions to enter the country's security and other bureaucracies. By the time U.S. forces readied to withdraw in December 2011, most central institutions, particularly those of defense, national security and economy were solidly in the hands of the pro-Iranians. If the Bush administration made several mistakes while trying to contain Iranian influence, it is safe to state that the Obama administration surrendered Iraq to the Iranian regime. The matter, as of 2009, was not an error in policy but policy itself. Washington's negotiations with the Iraqi government, led by Tehran's friends, projected the extension of Iran's influence across Iraq. While Congress expressed concerns under the Obama administration regarding Iraq slipping under Iranian influence, Washington's foreign policy establishment had already consented to have Iranian influence inside Iraq after the withdrawal. The main reason behind that consent, as it appears clear in 2014, is the long sought "deal" with the Ayatollahs' regime. Iranian influence over Iraq seems to have been part of a grand bargaining between the Obama administration and the Ayatollahs. Iran would cease its hostilities towards the U.S. in return for influence in Iraq and a zone of alliances stretching to Syria and Lebanon. The Iranian intervention in Iraq, and by ripple effect in Syria and Lebanon, while decided by Tehran years ago, has now, unfortunately, been agreed upon –or tolerated- by Washington despite sanctions and the fact that terror groups operating in Iraq, such as Hezbollah and the Pasdaran, remain on U.S. terror lists. [xxvii]

Iranian Terror in Lebanon

Iran's regime onslaught in Iraq and Syria made no exception in Lebanon and continues to persevere. The Khomeinist penetration of Lebanon, as indicated earlier started almost as early as the conclusion of the Iran-Syria cooperation treaty at the hands of Ayatollah Khomeini and President Hafez Assad in 1980. The objective of Tehran in Lebanon, as has been the case in Iraq, was to link up with radical elements inside the Shia community in that country, grow a pro-Iranian network in several areas, and over time push for control of Lebanon's national security—under Syrian tutelage. It has been clear to historians and geopolitical analysts that without Syria's initial help in the 1980s, the Iranian regime would not have been able to dominate Lebanon, let alone launch Hezbollah in that country. For prior to and during the first years of the Lebanese civil war of 1975-1980, most of the Shia community was either following traditional secular leaders affiliated with leftwing parties or beginning to identify with Imam Mussa Sadr who, while being a Shia populist leader (who mysteriously vanished in Libya in 1978), never vouched for the Khomeinist model. Until the landing of the first units of Pasdaran in the northern Bekaa valley in 1980, coming through Syria, the bulk of the Shia community was considered moderate. [xxviii]

By June 1976, the Syrian Army had invaded parts of Lebanon, including the Bekaa Valley, the north and west and southern Beirut. When the Khomenist revolution seized Iran in 1979, the Syrian occupied areas of Lebanon included a large swath of terrain where Shia made up a majority. The Iranian intelligence quickly dispatched elements to link up with radical groups and offshoots of the Amal Movement in Eastern Lebanon, entering the country via the Lebanese-Syrian borders—all under Assad's control. Shia Lebanese leaders and clerics were recruited, many were sent to Tehran for indoctrination, and militias, social networks and mosque networks were formed—all under Iranian supervision. The result was the establishment of Hezbollah, a paramilitary and militant organization operating under direct sponsorship of the Iranian Supreme Guide in Tehran. [xxix]

Throughout the 1980s, Hezbollah—on Tehran instructions—launched bombings and suicide attacks against the Marines and French units in Beirut as well as against the U.S. embassy and seized Western hostages, even killing some. After the Syrian invasion of the last free enclave in East Beirut in October 1990 and full Syrian control of Lebanon's government since, Hezbollah was granted protection, support and international cover by the new Assad-dominated regime in Lebanon for the following 15 years. During that decade and a half, Hezbollah penetrated the country's institutions, transformed itself into a terror army, and expanded its cells and networks in Africa, Latin America and North America. Along with the Iranian intelligence, Hezbollah was involved in bombings in Argentina and Saudi Arabia and in training and arming Hamas in the Gaza Strip. By 2000, Hezbollah reached the international border with Israel in the south and rose as the primary terror organization in the country and the region. [xxx]

Toward the end of 2003, Hezbollah was called by Iran's regime to penetrate Iraq and launch assaults against U.S.-led Coalition forces as well as against Iraqi moderates and Iranian opposition activists across the country. Using their Arabic speaking ability, Hezbollah's operatives in Iraq trained Iraqi Shia radicals, organized local terror networks, and worked on advancing the influence of Iran in Iraq—even under American occupation. Hezbollah targeted U.S., British, other Coalition members, as well as Iraqi and Iranian citizens opposed to Iran's regime. The organization helped train the "Mahdi Army" and other terror groups in the country until the full withdrawal of U.S. and allied forces in 2010. The Hezbollah

Iraq "veterans" came back to Lebanon to participate in violent acts against Lebanon's anti-Syrian occupation movement and, later, against politicians and Lebanese citizens opposed to Assad and Hezbollah. Hezbollah then used its security and war experiences in Iraq on the more recent battlefields in Syria. [xxxi]

Iran's destructive role in Syria

As we noted earlier in the report, the Syrian civil war was addressed jointly by the Iranian led axis in the region. From the first days of the demonstrations in Der'a and other Syrian cities in March 2011, the Iranian-Syrian-Hezbollah "war room" was in session to address the threat. For to the Iranian regime, any trouble menacing Assad's stability—let alone security—is a menace against Iran's interests in Syria and against Khomeinist regional ambitions. Pasdaran commanders in Tehran saw the relentless demonstrations in Syria throughout 2011 as a stark reminder of the demonstrations in Tehran two years earlier. From an Islamic Republic perspective, there could not be any reform in Syria even if Assad would have been willing to consider them. The overarching interest of Iran is a passage from Iraq to the Mediterranean Sea. If this goal fails, and for any reason the Syrian regime collapses, it would generate a domino effect in the region and a serious threat to Iran's regime. A crumbling of Assad's government would mean the rise of an anti-Iranian regime in Damascus, an isolation of Hezbollah in Lebanon, and unbearable pressure on the pro-Iranian Maliki government in Iraq. Worse in the eyes of the regime's strategists, a revolution in Syria might inspire a revolution in Iran. Hence, from day one of the upheaval in Syria, Iran's regime was on the side of Assad fighting against his enemies.[xxxii]

Iranian involvement in Syria was the principal reason for the survival of the Assad regime. During 2011, the Alawi Baathist regime used its own forces to clamp down on the civil society revolt. However, talks about a possible political transition under Assad were undergoing. Ideas were floating about a new government—of which half would consist of the opposition. But Tehran pressured Assad to accept no concession. For the Pasdaran, any sharing of power with the opposition was out of question. Iran's regime killed even the smallest possibility for a political settlement. The Assad circle, feeling surrounded by the U.S. from Iraq, from Turkey and Jordan—and fearing a NATO strike a la Libya, was pressuring the dictator to avoid Gaddafi's fate. But Iranian intelligence counter pressures reassured Assad that the United States is leaving Iraq and soon enough land bridges would be established between Iran and Syria via the vacated territory. But by the end of the year, as the FSA was forming and the Syrian opposition was militarizing, the Assad regime escalated its suppression campaign using a wider array of weapons. After the completion of U.S. withdrawal from Iraq in the early part of 2012, Iranian assets emerged at a greater rate in Syria, using Iraq's land and air routes. By the fall of that year, Hezbollah's units had been called upon to fight alongside the Assad regime and to connect with the Pasdaran inside Syria. The Iranian involvement in Syria shot down any chance of a political settlement between Assad and the opposition. When President Obama called on the Syrian dictator to step down, talks were generated about a solution that would arrange for Assad to evacuate Damascus (either to the Alawi areas or outside the country), and the Syrian Army would maintain stability in the interim. This equation was also shattered by the intransigence of Tehran's rulers who sidelined any option which would not insure their strategic interests in the country. Assad was Iran's best ally; any weakening of the dictator or a Syria without Assad would be a profound loss for the Khomeinists. Hence Iranian intervention in Syria escalated to a point where the IRG and intelligence became the backbone of Assad's defense against the armed opposition, especially with the rise of Sunni extremist militias. [xxxiii]

Throughout 2013, Hezbollah's military involvement became crucial to the Syrian regime as the Jihadists of al Nusra and other Islamist militias overran Assad units in the north of the country and as FSA fighters had the upper hand in the south of the country. Iran ordered Hezbollah into battle on several fronts inside Syria, particularly at the town of Qussair. The battles fought by Hezbollah in that city provided an opportunity for the organization to claim victories on the ground giving credit to Tehran's Pasdaran and to the Quds force. Iran's military and security apparatus in Syria got stronger and more omnipresent with every month that passed. The lines of communication between Iran and Hezbollah in Lebanon crossed strategic channels through Syria which are defended directly by Iranian assets and allies. In addition, Tehran insures free oil and large sums of cash to the Syrian regime in order to maintain its viability. In return, the Ayatollahs' regime has become the regional protector and real negotiator of the Syrian crisis. The role of Tehran in Syria can be summarized in two components. First, it has become a strategic pillar for the military and security survival of the regime, and two, it has simultaneously become the obstructer to any peace in Syria. As demonstrated through the Geneva Talks process, Tehran has become the deal maker on Syria. It has been able to stop negotiations when it was apparent it would not obtain a guarantee to its presence and interests in the country, yet it has allowed these negotiations when Assad came under greater pressure. On the security level, the Pasdaran, Iranian intelligence and Hezbollah have been involved in assassinations, arrests, torture, and terrorism. These practices have reached a point where the Iranian role in Syria cannot survive unless the Assad regime continues to rule. For in the event of any significant change in Damascus, it is to be expected that the Iranian regime's assets in Syria will be destroyed and its leaders prosecuted if apprehended. Tehran has forged one bloody choice for itself in Syria: that is to continue the fight and perpetuate the oppression of the Syrian people. [xxxiv]

The practical and undeclared strategy of the Iranian regime in Syria, however, is to insure communication lines between Iran and Lebanon via Iraq and Syria. These communication lines connect the Shia areas of Iraq to Hezbollah dominated zones of Lebanon. Across Syrian territory, these axes traverse the country from East to West and connect the Iraqi Shia zones to both Damascus and the Alawi enclave in the northern part of the country. Iran's regime considers these passages as vital to the survival of its presence east of the Mediterranean. The Syrian regime's Alawi core, Hezbollah, and Iraqi militias are primarily tasked with maintaining and defending these lines by using any and all means at their disposal. The international community has not yet captured the essence of role the of the Iranian regime in Syria, which is, essentially, to create demographic changes in order to secure this regional line of communication between Iran and the Mediterranean Sea through the installation of regimes and militants who are faithful to Tehran. The humanitarian crises inside Syria—including mass refugee problems, ethnic cleansing, and the terrorization of communities—are fundamentally linked to securing the Tehran-Hezbollah axis from Iran to Lebanon with Syria and Iraq as strategic geopolitical bridges. [xxxv]

Tehran's designs in Iraq mirror those in Syria

The Khomeinist line to the Mediterranean is not only an Iranian goal in Syria, but also in Iraq. Since the withdrawal of U.S. forces at the end of 2011, Iranian intelligence assets as well as Hezbollah operatives increased their role in Iraq. The Iranian strategic presence in Iraq has been facilitated by the Maliki government, whose bureaucracy, including defense and intelligence, is sympathetic to and often penetrated by Iranian cadres. Tehran's influence in Iraq relies on several components. Its main allies are the Shia radical militias, one of which having been the Mahdi Army, but also core militants within other militias which have been trained or hosted inside Iran for years before the U.S. intervention in 2003, including Badr Brigade and SCIRI. However, in addition to Iraqi radical armed networks, both the Pasdaran and Hezbollah maintain a presence across the country, with three tasks: (1) to help the Maliki government fight the Sunni insurgency in the center, (2) to oversee the Iranian web of communications with the Assad regime through Iraq, and (3) to assist in targeting Iranian opposition presence on Iraqi soil.[xxxvi]

Tehran's immediate priority in Iraq, during and since the U.S. pullout from the country, was to eliminate the Iranian exiles' ability to organize and reach out to their mother country from their bases in Iraq. Indeed, the proximity of Iranian opposition presence in Iraq to Iran's populations is considered by the Khomeinist regime as the most dangerous threat of all. Beyond military strikes and economic sanctions, what can most weaken and destabilize the Iranian regime is an organized and well-coordinated opposition based across the border. Of all countries neighboring Iran, Iraq was the only country which received Iranian dissidents in large numbers who have formed organized networks—as was the case in Camp Ashraf. The latter, organized by opposition group MEK, has been considered a top danger by Iran's intelligence because of its perceived ability to constitute a core of Iranian resistance against the Ayatollahs. Since the U.S. invasion, pro-Iranian elements in Iraq attempted to attack the camp and lobbied for its removal to satisfy Tehran.[xxxvii] However, as parts of Iraq's civil society and politicians opposed the dismantling of Ashraf, U.S authorities kept the camp under their protection. But since the pullout in 2012, Baghdad's government, under Tehran's pressures, pursued a relentless campaign of harassment and suppression against the exiles' site until Ashraf was finally invaded and then evacuated. Iran's objective against its exiles was partially reached through the dismantling of the opposition's main center of operations. [xxxviii]Aside from targeting Iranian opposition across Iraq, Iranian intelligence and its local allies assist Baghdad in suppressing the Iraqi opposition under the aegis of "fighting terror." While it is a fact that al Qaeda and its Jihadi ilk have been active and are increasingly operating in Iraq, particularly since the American pull out and with the escalation of Jihadi activities in Syria, Iranian security activity in the country is not limited to al Qaeda. In fact experts are divided about the real role Tehran has had in hosting some elements of Bin Laden's network after 9/11. The comprehensive activities of the Iranian operatives in Iraq have been centered on protecting their influence in Mesopotamia and striking at Iraqi opposition resisting their presence and role. In short, while many segments of Government and bureaucracies in Iraq are patriotic and are committed to fight the Jihadi terrorists, the national security command and control of the country, outside Iraqi Kurdistan, has fallen into the hands of the regional Iranian dominated axis. [xxxix]

Regime failure: Growing discontent

From 1979 until 2014, the Khomeinist regime has been successful at times in acquiring weapons, exerting influence, eliminating opponents, and expanding its reach in the region and beyond. It has also been somewhat successful in outmaneuvering Western powers, often escaping sanctions, and conducting propaganda warfare to survive amidst a constant domestic opposition. However, one area the regime systematically failed to administer has been to meet the basic demands and aspirations of its own people. Unlike Chile where the military regime had suppressed its citizens under the Pinochet regime yet produced a relatively successful economy, or South Africa's Apartheid regime which elevated the national economy to higher standards though at the price of an unacceptable human discrimination, the Ayatollahs' regime failed on both counts. On the one hand, it erected an extremely oppressive regime in Iran where freedoms, both political and social, vanished; and on the other hand, the national economy has grown unsuccessful, hopeless and dangerous for the social fabric of the country.

Tehran's elite failed to provide fundamental justice, protect public liberties, and manage the nation equitably. The Vilayet e Faqih, the supreme theological institution of the country—installed by the Islamic revolution that came after the collapse of the Shah regime—is based on a doctrine that cannot insure human rights, democracy and pluralism. By essence, the Supreme Guide doctrine is totalitarian as its legitimacy is based on divine mandate imposed by political elite. The Iranian regime belongs to categories of the medieval theologies of the Caliphates, Sultanates and absolute monarchies of post-Roman Europe, not to a 20th and 21st century government. The Khomeinists are in fact a Shia form of the Taliban, their Islamic Republic being a form of an Emirate with Western titles. The presidency, cabinet, members of the legislature, justice system, military and all other institutions are subjected to the unlimited theological power of the Vali e-Faqih. Such regimes cannot meet the requirements of a modern era representative government, nor are they able to materialize democratic choices and personal freedoms. And as argued above, the level of political suppression has been among the highest on the planet. This suppression, terror and torture have produced deep resentment within the Iranian people, manifested at several occasions inside the country and expressed by the exiled opposition. The regime has lost its moral and political legitimacy among most Iranians—those not connected financially to the core of the ruling elite.[xl]

In addition to freedom suppression, the Khomeinists have failed in providing basic economic needs to the general population of Iran. Over the past two decades, financial and socio-economic crises have been striking Iranians of all backgrounds and sectors of the country. The economic gap between the people and the regime has been increasingly growing, creating a two-class system in the country. A thorough analysis of Iran's socioeconomic system shows that the country has developed two economies, the one of the people and the one of the regime. From the bureau of the Supreme Guide to the Pasdaran, various and complex financial entities—the web of interests surrounding the ruling elite and those serving it—have created a closed economical system of its own, separated from the rest of the citizens.[xli]

It is to noteworthy that the regime has increased the frustrations of the public to new heights by failing to attend to its needs while at the same time keeping the elite financially well off. The wedge has been growing significantly over the past decade, especially as biting sanctions have been hurting the ability of the regime to provide the minimum to people. Shortages, corruption, embezzlements, and mismanagement have almost destroyed the economic infrastructure of the country. The international sanctions have hit the least protected parts of society and have at the same time demonstrated that Tehran's political elite cannot protect its own citizens economically while it has insulated itself as a regime from the effects of economic hardship.[xlii]

The present deteriorating socio-economic conditions are recipe for regime instability and vulnerability. The demonstrations of 2009 have shown how daring the masses have become, particularly the youth. However, the abandonment by the West and the U.S. of what could have been an Iranian upheaval has given the regime time and reassurances that it can repress the popular opposition at will. Regardless of U.S. abandonment of the protesters in June 2009, however, it is clear to observers and analysts that a deep fissure has been underway over the past five years inside the country. The image of Khamenei's ultimate power broker in the country has been irreversibly damaged. In short, the "Supreme Guide" and the Pasdaran know well that the popular mood is not on their side. In fact, the regime is at his weakest point in terms of popular legitimacy and is experiencing a pre-Arab Spring syndrome. Tehran understands that a successful revolt could bring down the regime or disorganize it: Which explains why the ruling elite and its supporting networks is escalating its domestic suppression and expanding its war mongering in the region. Oppressive regimes become more aggressive when they discover that their legitimacy has been exposed.[xliii]

U.S. new policies towards Iran's regime are needed

In view of the identification of Iran's strategic role in the region, particularly regarding its own population, and the countries of Iraq, Syria and Lebanon, the main question remaining is to determine the best paths for U.S policy regarding the Iranian regime.

The Obama administration, in its first and second terms, has committed strategic mistakes in the Middle East which will undermine U.S. national and security interests for many years, even under subsequent administrations after 2016.xliv The damage done is severe, and a remedy seems out of reach unless earth shattering changes are applied to Washington's foreign policy—either under the incumbent's administration or the next. The common core of U.S. strategic mistakes has been the perception of partners in the region since day one of the post-Bush presidency. While Bush's narrative on backing pro-democracy forces was right on track, the bureaucracy's actions betrayed the White House's global aim. By the time the Obama administration installed itself on Pennsylvania Avenue in 2009 little had been accomplished by the Bush bureaucrats in regards to identifying these pro-democracy forces and supporting them. When the current administration replaced Bush, however, civil society groups in the Middle East were systematically abandoned—aid to their liberal forces was cut off and engagement with the radicals became priority. The mistakes of the Bush bureaucracy became the official policy of the Obama administration.xlv

Washington's "new beginnings" in the region moved American Mideast policy in a backward direction on two major tracks. The first derailment was to partner with the Muslim Brotherhood, not the secular NGOs, in an attempt to define the future of Arab Sunni countries. The second was to engage the Iranian regime, not its opposition, in attempt to define future relations with the Shia sphere of the region. These were strategic policy decisions planned years before the Arab Spring, not a pragmatic search for solutions as upheavals began. Choosing the Islamists over the Muslim moderates and reformers has been an academically suggested strategy adapted to potential interests—even though it represents an approach contrary to historically successful pathways.

In June 2009, President Obama sent a letter to Iran's Supreme Leader asking for "engagement." This move, coupled with Washington's abandonment of the civil revolt in Iran that same month, sent a comforting message to the ruling Khomeinists: The United States is retreating from containment and will not support regime change in Iran. That undeniably emboldened Tehran to go on the offensive in the region after less than a decade of status quo.[xlvi]

The nuclear program was boldly defended despite American and UN economic sanctions; Iranian penetration of Iraq deepened; support to Hezbollah escalated with a presidential visit to Lebanon by Ahmadinejad; and aggressive backing of pro-Iranian elements in Arabia was sustained. The Arab Spring revealed more assertive Iranian behavior as Pasdaran and Hezbollah militias were dispatched to Syria in support of the struggling Assad regime.[xlvii] Across the region, the Ayatollahs increased their support to regimes and organizations bent on crushing civil society uprisings and also clamped down on their own oppositions—both inside the country and abroad. Tehran used Washington's unending search for dialogue with the Ayatollahs as an opportunity to attack the exiled Iranian community inside Iraq, one of the best cards in the international community's hands to pressure the Iranian regime. The tragedy of dismantling Camp Ashraf ran parallel to a systematic persecution of Iranian dissidents who rose in 2009 against the mullahs. U.S. retreat from Iran's containment led to an unparalleled bleeding of the political opposition, the only long term hope for a real change in Iran.[xlviii]

The Obama administration's abandonment of Iran's people was made complete through Washington's dangerous deal with Tehran. After months of secret negotiations and immediately after abandoning the Syrian opposition to vie for themselves against Iranian-backed Assad forces towards the end of the summer, the U.S. administration announced an interim nuclear agreement with Iran. To the astonishment of Iran's opposition, not to mention Arab moderate governments, European countries including France, and a majority in Congress, the Obama administration began easing sanctions on Iran in return for a promise by the Khomeinist regime that it would lower its uranium production to an internationally acceptable level. Without any significant leverage on Tehran, having sidelined the Iranian opposition, the White House has no guarantees that Iran's regime is backing off from nuclear strategic weaponry. Worse, Washington started almost immediately to transfer billions of dollars from "frozen accounts" back to the Iran regime's coffers.[xlix]

From an initial conceptual strategic mistake, the Obama administration moved to implement the most dangerous component of the new policy: Not only ending economic and political pressure, but sending financial support to a terror regime still on the offensive in the region. The hundreds of millions of dollars already received by the Ayatollahs can be, and actually most likely are being, recycled through the Pasdaran into subversive operations against the country's liberal opposition, the Iranian exiles, Arab governments and U.S. interests worldwide. The "deal" will go down in history as one of the worst political acts in the West, second only to the signing of a piece of paper in Munich that claimed to be a deal to save the Peace. History has already taught the world, at a very high price, the consequences of dealing with devils.[1]

Nevertheless, we do believe that Washington still has the ability to produce effective change in its Middle East policy, particularly regarding Iran.[li] The Obama administration should perform a global reevaluation of its past strategies regarding the Ayatollahs' regime and restructure its alternative policies based on a new set of strategies.

RECOMMENDATIONS

1) On the "nuclear deal": This agreement was not reviewed or voted on by the U.S. Congress—in contrast with the U.S. decision regarding striking Assad based on chemical weapon use (which Congress did vote on). We recommend the administration send the agreement, even after having committed to execute the accords with Tehran, back to the U.S. Congress for a vote to authorize it, modify it or even cancel it if U.S. national interests suggest so.

Other recommendations and strategies include:

2) Maintaining the current sanctions on the regime and focusing their implementation particularly on the regime's elite and their associates;

3) Introducing a bill in Congress to slate foreign aid to the Iranian opposition institutions, those in exile and civil society underground groups inside Iran, with a particular focus on political recognition of the MEK and its allies in the NCRI, to mobilize the Iranian people, with the goal of pressuring the regime to cease its oppression and accept the principle of a referendum on the future of the country;

4) Restructuring U.S. policy's main objective on Iran to focus on regime change by peaceful means and via coherent and systematic support to the Iranian opposition;

5) Inviting leaders of the Iranian resistance and opposition movements to the White House and the U.S. Congress to elevate their international visibility and grant them moral and political support.

These five new strategic recommendations for a change in U.S. policy toward Iran should receive the backing of the Obama administration and the U.S. Congress and become a bipartisan commitment to the people of Iran in its struggle to rebuild a free, democratic and pluralistic Iran.

Walid Phares
July 14, 2014

Dr Walid Phares is the author of *The Coming Revolution: Struggle for Freedom in the Middle East* of 2010 and of the newly released *The Lost Spring: U.S Policy in the Middle East and Catastrophes to avoid (March 2014).*

---

[i] Thomas Erdbrikmarch, 'No Guarantee' of Final Nuclear Deal With Iran, E.U. Official Says,' *The New York Times,* March 9, 2014

[ii] Chris Mitchell,"Iran Nuclear Deal: Mission Accomplished or Mistake?" *CBN News,* November 25, 2013; Also from the author of the report, Walid Phares: Obama's greatest mistake, Augusta Free Press Feb. 27, 2014

[iii] See Raymond Tanter, "MeK, Iran and the War for Washington," The National Interest, September 16, 2011

[iv] See"Iranian Diaspora's Convention Expressed Support for Iranian Resistance, Rejected Rouhani as Part of the Ayatollahs' Regime" PR Newswire, February 8, 2014

[v] See Jamie M. Fly and Gary Schmitt, The Case For Regime Change in Iran: Go Big -- Then Go Home, Foriegn Affairs, January 17, 2012; also Melik Kaylan, "How A Regime Change In Iran

Would Transform The World," Forbes June 24, 2010.

[vi] A comprehensive approach to the Iranian revolution was developed in the author's book *The Coming Revolution: Struggle for Freedom in the Middle East,* Simon and Shuster, November 2010

[vii] March 15, 1987, Dar al Mashreq, Beirut

[viii] *Journal of Global Affairs,* October 1991

[ix] Jubin Goodarzi, "Iran and Syria" May 3, *Pakistan Defence*, 2013

[x] On the alliance see Jubin M. Goodarzi, *Syria and Iran: Diplomatic Alliance and Power Politics in the Middle East* (Library of Modern Middle East Studies) I.B Tauris Jul 7, 2009

[xi] See Marius Deeb, Syria, Iran, and Hezbollah: The Unholy Alliance and Its War on Lebanon (Herbert & Jane Dwight Working Group on Islamism and the International Order) Hoover Institution Press; 1st edition (August 1, 2013)

[xii] Michael Rubin, "Were mistakes made on Russia, Turkey, and Iran?" Commentary Magazine, March 18, 2014

[xiii] "Obama To Iran Green Revolution Dissidents: Drop Dead" Investors Magazine, editors, February 28, 2012; also "Iran Green Revolution sparked momentum across the Middle East, editors, The Examiner, February 20, 2011.

[xiv] In our book *The Coming Revolution: Struggle for Freedom in the Middle East* published in 2010, before the Arab Spring, we projected that the Iranian revolt of June 2009 and the Beirut Cedars Revolution of 2005 would eventually influence similar movements in the region

[xv] "Iran shows no hesitation about intervening in Syria," editors, The Washington Post; September 20, 2012

[xvi] We projected decades of Syrian-Iranian strategic alliance in an article titled "The Syrian-Iranian Axis" published in *Global Affairs: The Journal of American Geopolitics*, August 1992

[xvii] See Robin Wright, Sacred Rage, Simon and Schuster, 2001

[xviii] Reuters, "Syria's Assad to win, victory to be Tehran's too: Iran official" September 29, 2012

[xix] "Iran to deploy '4,000-strong force' to Syria as US military set to stay in Jordan" Russia Today, June 16, 2013

[xx] Agence France Press, "Iranian Military Chief: 'We Will Support Syria To The End', September 5, 2013

[xxi] "Iran to deploy '4,000-strong force' to Syria as US military set to stay in Jordan," Russia Today, June 16, 2013

[xxii] Waleed Abu al-Khair, "Iranian Regime Uses ISIL To Preserve Syria Interests," Eurasia Review, April 18, 2014

[xxiii] Paulo Casaca, The Hidden Invasion of Iraq, Acacias Publishing, 2008

[xxiv] See Hamid al-Bayati, "From Dictatorship to Democracy: An Insider's Account of the Iraqi Opposition to Saddam," University of Pennsylvania Press, 2011

[xxv] From the briefing by Member of the European Parliament Paulo Casaca to the anti-Terrorism Caucus of the US House of Representatives in October 2008 on "Iran influence in Iraq"

[xxvi] See "U.S. Diplomat: Iraq 'Not Going to Be Pushed Around' by Iran," Associate Press, December 19, 2009

[xxvii] See Robin Wright, Iranian Unit to Be Labeled 'Terrorist' Washington Post, August 15, 2007; also Walid Phares "Is Iran's Revolutionary Guard Iran's SS", The Cutting Edge News, September 4th 2007 ; also Patrick Goodenough, "House Bill Would Designate Iran's Revolutionary Guard As Terrorist Group" CNS News, February 28, 2013

[xxviii] See William Harris, "Lebanon: A History, 600-2011 (Studies in Middle Eastern History) Oxford University Press, 2012

[xxix] See Dominique Avon and Anas-Trissa Khatchadourian, Hezbollah: A History of the "Party of God" Harvard University Press; 2012

[xxx] See Fabian Bosoer and Federico Finchekstein, "Argentina's About-Face on Terror" The New

York Times, March 1, 2013

xxxi See Matthew Levitt , "Hezbollah: The Global Footprint of Lebanon's Party of God" Georgetown University Press, 2013

xxxii See Jubin M. Goodarzi, Syria and *Iran: Diplomatic Alliance and Power Politics in the Middle East (*Library of Modern Middle East Studies) I. B. Tauris, 2009

xxxiii See Alireza Nader, "Why Iran Is Trying to Save the Syrian Regime" US News and World Report, April 24, 2013

xxxiv See Marius Deeb, Syria, Iran, and Hezbollah: The Unholy Alliance and Its War on Lebanon, Hoover Institution Press; 2013

xxxv Christopher Anzalone, "Zaynab's Guardians: The Emergence of Shi`a Militias in Syria" Combatting Terrorism Center at West Point, Jul 23, 2013; also Samia Nakhoul, "Special Report: Hezbollah gambles all in Syria" Reuters, September 26, 2013; also "Iran Revolutionary Guards commander killed in Syria" Reuters, November 4, 2013

xxxvi See Majid Rafizadeh "Iraq will remain in Iran's sphere of influence" al Shaeq al Awsat, March 16, 2014

xxxvii See Hugh Shelton, "Betrayal at Camp Ashraf" *Washington Times,* September 19, 2013; also Carolyn Beckingham, "US and UN Turning a Deaf Ear to Camp Ashraf Tragedy?" *News Blaze*, December 6, 2013

xxxviii N. Umid, "Iranian commander: Attack on Camp Ashraf has strategic importance" Trend, September 8, 2013

xxxix Scott Peterson, "Questions grow over Iran's influence in Iraq" September 11, Christian Science Monitor, 2012

xl Raghida Dergham, "The Oppression of the Iranian Regime Destroys Its Aura," al Arabiya January 2, 2010; also Angus Stickler and Maggie O'Kane, "Iran's Revolutionary Guards point to fresh dissent within oppressive regime", The Guardian, June 10, 2010; also "Iran: Oppression is mounting on students" National Council of the Iranian Resistance, Office of Foreign Affairs May 24, 2013

xli Mark Gregory, "Expanding business empire of Iran's Revolutionary Guards" BBC, July 26, 2010

xlii Thomas Erdbrink, "In Iran, Hopes Fade for Surge in the Economy" The New York Times, March 20, 2014

xliii Ravi Somaiya, "Oppression Continues in Iran," Newsweek, September 2, 2010

xliv James Jay Carafano, "Obama's policies created new paths for Iranian expansion," Washington Examiner October 21, 2013

xlv Hassan Daioleslam, "The Pro-engagement Lobby and US Failure with Iran" The American Thinker, May 16, 2010

xlvi Christiane Amanpour, "Obama sent letter to Iran leader before election, sources say" CNN, June 24, 2009; also "Obama sent second letter to Khamenei", The Washington Times, Sept 3, 2009

xlvii Jonathan Saul and Parisa Hafezi, "Iran boosts military support in Syria to bolster Assad," Reuters, February 21, 2014

xlviii As we outlined in *The Lost Spring: US Policy in the Middle East and Catastrophes to Avoid*, Palgrave, March 2014

xlix Reuters, "Iran to get access to billions of dollars under atom deal: U.S." November 23, 2013

l "U.S. Senator Cruz: "Iranian regime remains a brutal and oppressive dictatorship that pursues nuclear weapons" Valley News, November 27, 2013

li "Iranian Opposition Leader: Western Countries Should Make Their Relations With Tehran Conditioned on Guaranteeing Human Rights," PR Newswire, April 12, 2014

www.ingramcontent.com/pod-product-compliance
Lightning Source LLC
Chambersburg PA
CBHW081757280526
45789CB00008B/2898